D1112651

Acknowledgments:
The author and publishers wish to thank the following for permission to use copyright material:
BBC Hulton Picture Library – pages 13, 25 (top left), 26 (top right), 28 (top), 29 (both), 43 (nos. 1 and 2), 50 (top); Camera Press (Baron) – page 46 (left); Central Press Photos – pages 17, 42; Country Life Books – cover and pages 9 (top), 12, 15, 37 (bottom), 41 (bottom); Fox Photos – pages 26 (bottom right), 27 (top and middle), 31 (top), 32, 34 (both), 35 (top), 36, 38 (both), 39 (nos. 4, 5, 6, 8), 40 (both), 43 (nos. 3, 5), 44 (both), 45 (nos. 3, 4, 5, 6), 47 (both), 48 (top), 50 (bottom); Imperial War Museum – pages 14 (top), 16 (top), 18 (top); Keystone Press – page 31 (bottom); Martyn Larkin – front endpaper (left), page 41; Keith Logan – title page and page 8; Mansell Collection – pages 22, 24, 25 (top right), 28 (bottom), 33 (nos. 1, 4); National Portrait Gallery – page 6 (left), 7, 18 (bottom), 19; Popperfoto – page 33 (nos. 2, 3, 5); R M Powell – family tree, back endpaper; Kevin Rook – page 20 (left), 39 (no. 3), 43 (no. 4); Scotsman Features Ltd – page 37; John Scott – front endpaper (right), pages 5, 35 (bottom), 39 (no. 7), 46 (no. 7), 46 (bottom), 48 (middle), 49, 51, and back cover; Space Frontiers Ltd – page 4 (bottom right); Syndication International – page 4 (top), 6 (bottom right), 10, 14 (bottom), 16 (bottom), 26 (top left), 27 (bottom).

© LADYBIRD BOOKS LTD MCMLXXXII

All rights reserved. No part of this publication may be reproduced, stored in a retrieval system, or transmitted in any form or by any means, electronic, mechanical, photo-copying, recording or otherwise, without the prior consent of the copyright owner.

HM Queen Elizabeth
The Queen Mother

by IAN A MORRISON MA PhD

Ladybird Books Loughborough

The 20th century has brought some of the greatest changes the human race has ever experienced. The story of the lady best known to us now as the Queen Mother begins with the century, and matches it in its blend of tragedies, delights and sheer surprises.

Since her birth in 1900, the number of people on Earth has more than doubled, but in other ways the globe has shrunk dramatically.

An early photograph of the Queen Mother

When she was little, steam boats and trains were the fastest ways of getting round the world. The first flight by a powered aircraft was still three years ahead when she was born, yet she was to see men walk upon the

After morning service at Windsor

Moon. To her parents the television set upon which she watched them would have seemed as unlikely a piece of science fiction as the notion of leaving the Earth by rocket... something out of story-books by Jules Verne or H G Wells *(far left)*, not something that might actually happen during their daughter's lifetime.

An old Scots song tells of 'a lad who was *born* to be king' (though that Prince Charlie fled 'Over the Sea to Skye', and never became a monarch). The baby girl who came into the world on 4th August 1900 was not born to Royalty, and though she married a Prince called Albert they did not expect to ascend the throne, because he was not the King's eldest son.

Children born to the Royal Family were brought up very strictly, with the idea of preparing them for life in the public gaze.

Prince Albert as a cadet

Lady Elizabeth Bowes-Lyon at the age of seven

An unusually informal photograph (for the time)
of the Bowes-Lyon family

Prince Albert was sent away to Naval college, and did not have a very happy childhood. In contrast, Elizabeth's parents valued the privacy of a relaxed home life, away from publicity. So she grew up in a warm family atmosphere. By reflecting this and by helping to shape the present-day Royal Family so that it is very clearly an affectionate family team, she has helped to give it the flexibility and durability that has kept it a popular part of the British scene in this changeable century.

The Queen Mother's coat of arms

If she was not born to be a Queen, this is not to
say that she lacked Royal blood. Robert the Bruce,
the King of Scots, was one of her ancestors. Her
family name is Bowes-Lyon (so their coat of arms is a
pictorial pun, with bows-and-arrows and lions...),
and ever since the time of 'The White Lyon', blond
Sir John of the 14th century, they have owned
Glamis Castle on the edge of the Highlands.

Like all the best castles, it has its share of ghost
stories. It is said that the Earl Beardie still likes to
sneak up on sleeping children to toss his whiskers
and rattle dice. One Lady Glamis really was burned
as a witch, and Shakespeare used the castle as his
setting for *Macbeth*.

Glamis Castle

Her family's roots are not only Scottish, but spread through the British Isles and beyond. In Wales they reach back to Owain Glendwr, one of the last independent warrior princes. The Bowes family relate her to both the North and South of England, while other strands link her to America, and even George Washington himself.

George Washington

9

Her full maiden-name was Elizabeth Angela Marguerite Bowes-Lyon. It is said that she was called Elizabeth after the Queen of Shakespeare's time; that her father chose Angela since he thought she was like a little angel (one wonders what rogueries his previous eight children had got up to, if number nine seemed the first angelic one!); and Marguerite arose from her mother's fondness for flowers, something her daughter inherited.

Although the family was an affectionate one, there was an age gap between Elizabeth and her brothers and sisters (the eldest was seventeen years older than she was). She might have become a lonely little girl, with nobody her own age to play with.

In August 1902, with her older sister (later Lady Elphinstone)

The Queen Mother's parents, the Earl and Countess of Strathmore

However, when she was just fifteen months old, she was joined in the nursery by a baby brother, David. They grew up together, almost like twins, and their mother used to call them 'her two Benjamins'. They were not always as 'angelic' as they tried to look.

A painting of Lady Elizabeth with her young brother David

St Paul's Walden Bury

Although they went to Glamis for part of each year, much of their childhood was spent where she had been born, at their family home of St Paul's Walden Bury in the countryside just north of London. Her mother, Lady Strathmore, told them that if you found anything or anybody a bore, the fault was in yourself.

For children encouraged to use their imagination, there was little danger of boredom in the enchanted woods, full of ponds and primroses, around the Georgian house. Even the statues among the wild strawberries became characters (they called the Discus Thrower the 'Bounding Butler') while the cooing ring-doves in the big oak were dubbed Caroline-Curley-Love and Rhoda-Wrigley-Worm. When a pig they knew, called Lucifer, was offered as a prize in a village raffle, Elizabeth and David saved

up and managed to buy up nearly half the tickets. But they never saw him again. Sometimes they would disappear too. When they were five and six they used to escape morning lessons by hiding in the attic of an old outhouse, where they kept a secret store of apples and chocolates. The ladder was so rotten that it would not take the weight of Nanny. They were safe from pursuit, but the fleas from the hens were a problem up there.

In fancy dress —
Lady Elizabeth and her
brother David, 1909

13

Trench warfare at Ypres, 1917

They were rogues at Glamis too. They 'defended the Castle' by pouring 'boiling oil' from the ramparts onto 'invaders'. Though it was just a tubful of cold water, it was still a bit of a shock for innocent visitors.

But soon the family was affected by the sadness of a real conflict. On Elizabeth's fourteenth birthday, the First World War broke out. Her elder brothers went away to the army, and Fergus was killed in the battle of Loos. Then Michael was reported dead too. His body was not found and David dreamed that he was still alive but badly hurt. After three months, word came that he was in an enemy prison hospital, with a head wound.

Lady Elizabeth shakes hands with one of the wounded soldiers who convalesced at Glamis Castle

Glamis Castle became a hospital for British wounded, and Elizabeth spent most of her teenage years there, helping with the nursing. As one soldier put it, she was 'great medicine'. Lively and kindly, she sang with them, fetched messages from the village and took photographs for them to send home. She grew up quickly during the years of war, taking on more and more responsibility as her mother's health failed.

Then when the Castle caught fire one dark December night, she showed that she had the nerve and leadership to cope with a full-scale emergency too.

HMS Barham

Shortly after peace had returned, a party was held aboard HMS *Barham*. Though the guests were all very distinguished, in the eyes of the young Midshipmen they were also very old. The only visitor of their own age was a certain Lady Elizabeth Bowes-Lyon, so there was great competition for her company. She asked why one of them was pacing the quarterdeck with a telescope under his arm and a worried look on his face, instead of

16

joining in the dancing. Another explained that his friend was Midshipman of the Watch, and being on duty he wouldn't even get a sniff at the refreshments. 'Poor chap' she said...and a plot was hatched. He was fed through a porthole with sandwiches and champagne, and the future Queen of England gained the devotion of several future subjects.

It was about then that the path that was to lead her to the throne began to open before her, though she could not know that. Through Girl Guide work, she had become a friend of Princess Mary, and was invited to the Palace. There she re-met the King's second son, Prince Albert, Duke of York.

Lady Elizabeth Bowes-Lyon in Girl Guide uniform

HMS Collingwood

Elizabeth and Albert had met once before, at a children's party when she was five. He was friends with her brothers, and like them he served in the war. He was manning a gun-turret when HMS *Collingwood* fought off enemy cruisers and destroyers in the Battle of Jutland. His coolness under fire was noted both officially and unofficially (the gun-crew recalled young Albert making cocoa for them, just as usual). He enjoyed both study and sport, and as well as going to Cambridge University, he qualified

Prince Albert as a midshipman

as a pilot and became the first Royal entrant at Wimbledon.

He was thus a brave and capable person, but he had grown up to be a very shy boy, with a difficult stammer. What has been called the unrelieved starchiness of Court life made it difficult for the older Royalty to get on with children. Lady Asquith recalls that little Bertie once tried several times to interrupt the grown-ups' conversation. King Edward VII ordered 'Don't talk, my boy, until we have finished luncheon!' When the gruff old King finally asked what he had wanted to say, Albert had to admit, 'It doesn't matter now, Grandpapa. I was going to tell you there was a caterpillar in your salad, but you've eaten it.'

Prince Albert (right) in flying clothes

'Unrelieved starchiness' was hardly the style of the household in which the Lady Elizabeth grew up, and it is clear that Prince Albert enjoyed his visits to Glamis and St Paul's Walden Bury. But the difference between her family and the stiffness of the Royal household must have been something that she worried about, however

much she liked Prince Albert. On the one side was privacy and friendliness, on the other the harsh light of publicity, and very possibly loneliness. After all, it would be the first time since the 17th century that a son of a British King had married a commoner, instead of a wife who was royal in her own right.

When he first asked her to marry him, she was just twenty and she did not accept. However, two years later on the quiet Sunday morning of 14th January 1923, they strolled through winter groves in her 'enchanted woods' of St Paul's, and decided that they would get married.

The 'enchanted woods' at St Paul's Walden Bury

On the balcony — after the wedding *In the famous Glass Coach*

21

The bride and groom, with their in-laws

Becoming a member of the Royal Family did bring pressures, but becoming the King's daughter-in-law worked out very happily. George V felt he had to be very strict in bringing up Princes, but since he did not expect Albert to become king, he did not have to think of her as a future queen. He was pleased to accept her as the lively girl she was.

When he died, twelve years later, it is said that she wrote to his old doctor saying that she missed him dreadfully...and that, unlike his own children, she was never afraid of him...he was always ready to listen and give advice. And when he was in the mood, she wrote, he could be deliciously funny too!

She could understand an old king whose sense of duty made him INSIST (not very successfully in her case!) that the Family should never be late for breakfast...but who then allowed his pet parrot Charlotte to raid the marmalade. After all, when she was little, a Bullfinch called Bobby had shared her plate (and free-flying budgerigars would startle visitors to her home, when she was a grandmother).

The Duchess of York with her father-in-law, King George ▼

Prince Albert was Duke of York, and as Duchess of York she was plunged with him into the extraordinarily varied round of duties of the Royal Family. Some of these are solemn, and are concerned with presenting Britain to the world with a unity and dignity that is difficult for politicians to match amid the squabbles of their party politics. But there is a less solemn side too. Part of the success of the Royal Family in helping to bind together the peoples of United Kingdom and Commonwealth has come from their ability to share friendliness and humour, in a way that ordinary families appreciate. This is a lot less easy than it seems, because the constant pursuit by newsmen and the publicity over their every action makes it difficult to be at all natural, particularly for a shy person like Prince Albert.

But as the old King wrote to him, 'You are indeed a lucky man... I am quite certain that Elizabeth will be a splendid partner in your work...' and so it proved.

Glamorous for a formal occasion

Trying her hand at a coconut shy   *A wounded soldier jokes with her*

She helped him to overcome his stutter. But more
important, her own character soon shone through,
and broke the ice for them both with the public.

*The ceremony of 'Crossing the Line' (the Equator) on HMS Renown
– even the Duke and Duchess must submit to the fun!*

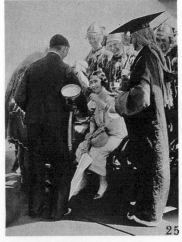

25

At the Wembley Exhibition in 1925   At Darlington

They were soon meeting that public all over
Britain and all round the world, in their role as
Royal ambassadors. Travel by land, sea and air has
been a constant feature of her life since then. They
were amongst the first of the Royal Family to take
regularly to the air. At first this was in canvas-
covered biplanes, but in later life she was to try her
hand at the controls of a jet in the stratosphere, and
to have grandsons who flew helicopters and 1600 kph
jet fighters.

Arriving at Edinburgh Airport

The Duchess takes to the air for
the first time

The Royal Yacht Britannia

But much of her travel was at a more sedate rate, and amid the hurly-burly of public engagements, she must have appreciated the chance of a little peace and privacy that she could enjoy on the Royal Yacht, or on some (though not all!) trains.

On Britannia — the sitting room

The Duke of York drives a model train at a bazaar

On the lawn at Windsor

Their first daughter, who was to become Queen Elizabeth, was born in London on 21st April 1926, and their second, Princess Margaret Rose, at Glamis on 21st August 1930. This meant that they were eleven and six years old before their father and mother were unexpectedly made King and Queen. Instead of taking Court life as their model, their parents looked on family life as a sanctuary in which people could develop despite the pressures on them in the outside world.

The happiness of her own early days seems to have guided the way she and her husband decided to bring up their own family. This is important, because the pattern of family life that she set with Albert then, in the ten years before they were aware that they would come to the throne, has been continued through to her grandchildren's generation.

With Princess Elizabeth and the Earl of Airlie

At Royal Lodge, Windsor

Many people feel that this feeling of the Royal Family being a real family has contributed a lot to their continuing popularity in the last part of the 20th century.

Relaxing at Windsor

When the old King died on 20th January 1936, his oldest son was proclaimed King Edward VIII. But he was never to be crowned. In the face of great hostility from politicians and others over whom he might marry, he decided to abdicate: that is, to give up his right to the throne.

So, quite suddenly Prince Albert found that he was required to become a Sovereign. He was to be known as King George VI, and his wife would become his Queen Consort.

They were crowned in Westminster Abbey on 12th May 1937. The two little Princesses were there, dressed in white and gold, and appeared afterwards with their parents on the balcony of Buckingham Palace.

A solemn moment

After the coronation in 1937 — a balcony appearance

At Buckingham Palace, World War II

They all had to put a brave face on it, but the change was not of their choosing. The new King had not gone through the training of a Prince of Wales, and he told Lord Mountbatten he felt quite unprepared to take over the affairs of State. However, as his brother had said during his abdication speech, '..he has one matchless blessing...not bestowed on me — a happy home life.' And as he came to the throne, he left no doubt of the value he set on this: 'With my wife and helpmate by my side, I take up the heavy task which lies before me.'

They needed all their family fortitude, for soon the country was looking to them to inspire steadfastness and hope through the long years of the Second World War. The King and Queen refused to leave the capital, though the Palace was hit nine times by bomb and rocket attacks.

1 *The Queen takes bananas to children injured in a bombing raid*
2 *The King and Queen tour East London in 1945*
3 *Inspecting the damage to Buckingham Palace*
4 *The Queen talks to two Canadian soldiers*
5 *With Winston Churchill on Victory Day 1945*

1947 – This Royal Family group included Lieutenant Philip Mountbatten, Princess Elizabeth's fiancé

By the time the War ended in 1945, King George and Queen Elizabeth could be in no doubt that they had earned the affection of their people. This was a happy period for the whole family. First, Princess Elizabeth married the young Philip Mountbatten, who became the Duke of Edinburgh. Then in April of 1948, her parents celebrated their own Silver Wedding, before their first grandchild, Prince Charles, was born in November. Their second, Princess Anne, arrived in August 1950.

A Silver Wedding picture

The King found as much pleasure with his grandchildren as he had with his own daughters. But serious illnesses had troubled him ever since he was a boy, and although he was still only in his fifties, problems with leg arteries and then a malignant lung growth weakened him seriously. Besides taking over many of his Royal duties, his wife worked with the nurses and doctors. She helped to see him through days and nights of crisis, just as she had helped others with the nursing so long before, when she was a girl at Glamis.

A happy afternoon on the moors in 1949

The funeral of King George VI at Windsor Castle

King George VI died in February 1952, leaving her a widow at just fifty one years of age. As Queen Consort, a commoner married to a King, she did not succeed him. So it was her daughter who came to the throne, through the Blood Royal of her father the late King. Because they both were Elizabeths, the parent henceforth became known officially as Her Majesty Queen Elizabeth The Queen Mother: and as years went by, unofficially (though certainly not unaffectionately) as The Queen Mum...

The Castle of Mey

The Queen Mother had not expected to become a Queen at all, and in the sadness following her husband's death she might have retreated into the kind of quiet country life her own family had enjoyed. When she started making a home out of the old Castle of Mey, in one of the furthest corners of her native Scotland, people wondered if she was going to retire there for good.

But once the first sorrow had passed she set out, as she put it, to continue the work that she and her husband had sought to do together. For thirty years since then, the affection in which she has been held by people in Britain and many other parts of the world has ensured that she has been kept a busy person. She has been involved in an extraordinary range of activities, always seeming to manage to approach events great and small (from chats with individuals through to great formal occasions) with her own pleasant and highly personal style.

1 *Opening a biology laboratory at Queen Mary College*
2 *At Belfast University*
3 *Presenting a shamrock to the Irish Guards*
4 *At the Royal Opera House, Covent Garden*
5 *Meeting Petula Clark*
6 *At the opera*
7 *An unexpected skill!*
8 *At Dover, as Warden of the Cinque Ports*

Clarence House

Even into her seventies and eighties, her days have stayed well filled. Her diary of engagements is planned for months ahead. Even moments of repose are turned to use: there have generally been at least half a dozen artists waiting their turn to paint her portrait, so few days have passed without her sitting for someone. Each public event has involved not only the time spent in making the appearance itself, and in getting back and forth, but quite a lot of homework on whom she is meeting, what they do, and what their

This portrait was painted for the Royal College of Music by Sir Leonard Boden

interests are. On top of this there are all the private business meetings with people from the organisations she has helped.

With pressure like this as a routine fact of life, her London home of Clarence House only seems so serene a place because of the quiet efficiency of her personal household. Many of them have grown old together, some being with her for as much as forty years — which surely says a lot about her personality.

At a Flower Show in Windsor Great Park

At her desk

She has had her own favourite forms of relaxation that must have helped her to cope with the stresses of such a long public life.

One of these has been fishing. Angling probably attracts the greatest number of people who actually take part in any sport in Britain (as opposed to those who just watch others playing). The thousands of people who share in it know how restorative a day out with a rod can be...even if it does rain, and the big one gets away! She has been an angler since her early days in Scotland, and when Prince Charles was a boy, she taught him fly-fishing there too.

Another enthusiasm that has run right through her life has been for horses. The family interest in riding goes back long before Princess Anne and Prince Charles. When she was little, her tiny Shetland pony, Bobs, sometimes found his way indoors (and indeed upstairs...) Even as a great-grand-mother, she has kept a lively interest in the stables where the Royal horses are trained, as well as following their fortunes at the races.

A favourite sport

1   As a girl, on Bobs a much-loved pony

2   Royal Lodge

3   Presenting a cup at Sandown Park

4, 5   At the races

Not surprisingly after the special magic of those 'enchanted woods' of Walden Bury, gardens have always been something that she has cared about. Her mother was an expert gardener, and then she and Albert spent some of their happiest times together remodelling the garden of the Royal Lodge at Windsor, which has remained a favourite place of hers all her life.

And having enjoyed her own childhood, at Walden Bury and at Glamis, and enjoyed bringing up her daughters, she has had a better understanding than many grown-ups of how to get on with children. It has not been just a matter of being good with those she has met on her travels. It is clear that as Grannie and then Great-Grannie she has been a rather special person to the successive generations of Royal children.

1 *On the way to morning service at Sandringham*
2 *Visiting a school*
3 *With her grandchildren on her 60th birthday*
4 *At the christening of Princess Anne's son*

5 *At Chelsea
   Flower Show*
6 *Opening a
   Gardening Centre
   in Middlesex*
7 *At Braemar*

45

She has certainly always had a special relationship with her first grandson, Prince Charles. Growing up can have its problems, whoever you are. As the first heir to the British throne to be sent out to a public school, he had to face extra pressures, and it is said that her wiseness helped him through some

At the christening of Prince Charles

of the rougher patches. From the time when his grandmother towered over him, until he grew to tower over her, they have clearly remained good friends. She used to tell the children stories, and it's nice to find him taking over the family tradition and spinning the younger ones yarns set in the vastnesses of the Scottish Highlands — where she had first heard of dread Earl Beardie, when she was a little girl...

A schoolboy Charles with his grandmother

(Above) *After the ceremony of the*
Order of the Garter, at Windsor

(Left) *At the Royal College of Music*

Sandringham House

Now Prince Charles is married, and one wonders whether in the best tradition of fairy tales his grandmother may have been something of a Fairy Godmother too. The Lady Diana Spencer was 'the girl next door', born at Park House next to the Royal Family's country home at Sandringham, and all the generations knew each other well. *Her* grandmother had been one of *his* grandmother's Ladies-in-Waiting and companions for many years.

At the Hon. Nicolas Soames' wedding

Although over six decades separate the Princess of Wales and the Queen Mother, they are not dissimilar in some ways. Although not born as Princesses, both are from families close enough to the crown to realise what was involved in joining the Royal Family. Both are lively, open-air persons, with a love of music, and a very special place in their hearts for children...

Christmas 1981

When the little girl who was eventually to become Queen Elizabeth The Queen Mother was born in 1900, many more countries had Royal Families. Some of these still had very real power over their people. Today, after the turmoil of two World Wars, most countries have other forms of rule. In a few however, a special kind of partnership has evolved. In this the main power to govern has passed to the elected representatives of the people, but the Royal Family has become a special symbol for the nation as a whole, both at home and in the eyes of the world.

The extent to which this partnership has succeeded in the United Kingdom was brought out not only by the popularity of the Royal Wedding of 1981, but by the long-standing affection of the British for their Queen Mother. Perhaps more than any other single person, she can be given the credit for the way that an attractive version of Royalty, appropriate for the 1980s, has evolved through all the changes the world has seen this century.

At Clarence House, 1975

51

Family Tree

PATRICK (LYON),
3rd EARL of STRATHMORE & KINGHORNE
Born 1643
Died 1695

Lady HELEN MIDDLETON
Married 1662
Died 1708

JOHN (LYON),
4th EARL of STRATHMORE & KINGHORNE
Born 1663
Died 1712

Lady ELIZABETH STANHOPE
Married 1691
Died 1723

THOMAS (LYON),
8th EARL of STRATHMORE & KINGHORNE
Born 1704
Died 1753

JEAN NICHOLSON
Married 1736
Died 1778

JOHN (LYON),
9th EARL of STRATHMORE & KINGHORNE,
Born 1737
Died 1776

MARY ELEANOR BOWES
Married 1767
Died 1800

THOMAS (BOWES-LYON),
11th EARL of STRATHMORE & KINGHORNE
Born 1773
Died 1846

MARY ELIZABETH CARPENTER
Married 1800
Died 1811